A FIRST BIBLE

A FIRST BIBLE

New Testament

Illustrations by Letizia Galli

Adapted by Toby Forward from an original
French text by François Brossier and
Danielle Monneron

S I M O N   &   S C H U S T E R

LONDON•SYDNEY•NEW YORK•TOKYO•TORONTO

First published in Great Britain by
Simon & Schuster Limited 1989

**Simon & Schuster Limited, West Garden Place,
Kendal Street, London W2 2AQ**

Simon & Schuster Australia Pty Limited
Sydney, New South Wales

Distributed in Canada by:
General Publishing Ltd. (trade)
30, Lesmill Road, Don Mills, Ontario, M3B 2T6

Novalis (religious)
P.O. Box 9700, Terminal, Ottawa, Ontario K1G 4B4

Originally published in France by Éditions du Centurion, Paris,
under the title *Ma Première Bible en Images*.

British Library Cataloguing in Publication Data

Brossier, François.
  A First Bible.
    1. Bible. N.T.
    I. Title   II. Monneron, Danielle   III. Galli,
    Letizia   IV. Bible. N.T. English. Selections: 1989
    V. Ma première Bible en images. English
    225

    ISBN 0-671-69680-7

Typeset in Helvetica by Opus, Oxford
Printed in France

Introduction

The Bible is a difficult and complicated book, especially for children. It is important, though, for even the youngest child to have access to the scriptures that have been handed down from generation to generation.

In this volume of the New Testament of *A First Bible* the main stories from the life of Christ are told in simple text and radiant illustrations. It is desirable that young children should encounter Jesus first through the great accounts of the Gospels. The four Gospels of the New Testament however, do not claim to represent a chronological history but rather are four portraits of Jesus, each with its own characteristics. There is, therefore, no question of mixing them together. For this reason, as far as possible, *A First Bible* stays within one single Gospel for each of the great events in the life of Jesus: his Childhood, Ministry, Preaching, Passion and Resurrection.

Following on from the volume of the Old Testament, the New Testament uses a narrative style as the form most suited to the understanding of very young children. Even so, the texts that are retained cannot reflect the whole of the New Testament, since parts are difficult to represent using key words and pictures. It is hoped that children will build on this first encounter with the Bible right through their education.

At the end of the book, stories from the New Testament are retold for children and allow links to be made between each of the illustrated pages. Parents should also not hesitate to read their children the actual Gospels themselves. *A First Bible*, both Old and New Testament, is intended not as a replacement for reading the Bible but rather as an aid to a child's first approach to it.

young girl

The Angel Gabriel was sent by God

to a town called Nazareth, to a

young girl.

The girl's name was Mary.

The angel said to her,

'You will have a son, and his name is

to be Jesus.'

Luke 1:26,27,31

manger

Mary brought her son, her first born,

into the world in Bethlehem,

the city of David.

She laid him in a **manger** because

there was no room for them inside

the inn.

Luke 2:4,7

shepherds

There were **shepherds** in the fields,

taking care of their sheep.

The Angel of the Lord appeared to them

and said,

'I have come to bring you good news.

Today a Saviour has been born for you.

He is the Messiah, the Lord.'

Luke 2:8,9,10,11

new-born baby

The shepherds found Mary and Joseph,

with the **new-born baby**

lying in a manger.

Luke 2:16

star

Wise men from the east came to

Jerusalem and asked,

'Where is the new-born King of the Jews?

We have seen his **star**.'

Matthew 2:1,2

gold, frankincense
and myrrh

King Herod sent them to Bethlehem.

They saw the child with Mary his mother,

and they gave him their gifts:

gold, frankincense and myrrh.

Matthew 2:8,11

sword

His parents took Jesus to Jerusalem

to present him to the Lord.

There was a man there called Simeon.

He blessed them and then he said to Mary,

'Your son will cause the fall

and the revelation of many things.

He will be a sign of division.

And as for you, a **sword** will

pierce your heart.'

Luke 2:22,25,34,35

child

The **child** grew strong and wise.

God's grace blessed him.

Luke 2:40

pilgrimage

Every year

Jesus' parents went to Jerusalem

for the feast of the Passover.

When he was twelve years old

they made the **pilgrimage** in the

usual way.

The young Jesus stayed in Jerusalem and

his parents did not notice that he

was missing.

Luke 2:41,42,43,44

temple

They found him in the **Temple**

three days later.

He said to them,

'Didn't you know I would be in my

Father's house?'

Luke 2:46, 49

desert

John the Baptist came to the **desert**.

He said,

'Watch. A man is coming after me

who is greater than I am.'

Mark 1:4,7

water

Jesus came from Nazareth
and was baptized by John
in the **water** of the Jordan.

Mark 1:9

dove

As soon as he came out of the water,

Jesus saw the Spirit come down on him

like a **dove**.

A voice said,

'You are my beloved son.'

Mark 1:10,11

fishermen

Walking alongside the sea of Galilee,

he saw two **fishermen**, Simon and his

brother Andrew, casting their nets.

Jesus said to them,

'I will make you fishers of men.'

They followed him immediately.

Mark 1:16,17,18

twelve

Jesus went up the mountain
and he called the ones he
wanted to him.
They came with him
and he appointed **twelve**
of them to be with him.

Mark 3:13,14

marriage

There was a **marriage** at Cana in Galilee.

Jesus and his mother were there.

John 2:1,2

jars

The wine ran out.

Jesus' mother said to the servants,

'Do everything he tells you.'

Jesus said to the servants,

'Fill the **jars** with water.'

John 2:3,5,7

wine

Jesus said to them,

'Draw some out and take it

to the steward of the feast.'

The steward of the feast tasted the water

turned into **wine**.

This was the first of the signs of Jesus.

He showed his disciples his glory and they

believed in him.

John 2:8,9,11

paralytic

The news spread

that Jesus was at the house.

Some people arrived carrying

a **paralytic** man on

a stretcher.

Mark 2:1,3

stretcher

Because they could not get near

to him for the crowd

they stripped off the roof

and lowered down the **stretcher**.

Mark 2:4

get up

Jesus said to the paralytic,

'**Get up**. Take your stretcher

and go home.'

Mark 2:11

brothers

Then his mother and his **brothers** arrived.

The people said to him,

'Your mother and your

brothers are outside here,

looking for you.'

He said to them,

'Who is my mother?

Who are my brothers?

Whoever does God's will is my brother, my

sister, my mother.'

Mark 3:31,32,33,35

boat

That day, when evening had come,

he said to his disciples,

'Let us sail over to the other shore.'

They took Jesus in the **boat**.

Mark 4:35,36

storm

A violent **storm** rose up.

The waves threw themselves against the boat.

But Jesus was sleeping on a cushion in

the stern.

Mark 4:37,38

calm

His disciples woke him up.

He commanded the wind and the sea

to be still.

The wind dropped and there

was a great **calm**.

They said to one another,

'Who is this man?'

Mark 4:38,39,41

crowd

When he disembarked Jesus saw a

great **crowd**.

His disciples said,

'This place is a desert and it is already late.

Send them away so that they can go and buy

something to eat.'

Mark 6:34,35,36

loaves

He replied:

'Give them something yourselves.

How many **loaves** do you have?'

They told him,

'Five, and two fishes.'

Mark 6:37,38

blessing

Jesus took the five loaves and the two fishes.

Raising his eyes to heaven

he spoke the **blessing**,

broke the loaves

and gave them to his disciples

to distribute.

Mark 6:41

baskets

All ate until they were satisfied.

And they collected twelve **baskets**

full of the scraps that were left.

Mark 6:42,43

mountain

Jesus took Peter, James and John with him

and led them to the top of a high **mountain**.

He was transfigured in their sight,

and his clothes shone.

Mark 9:2,3

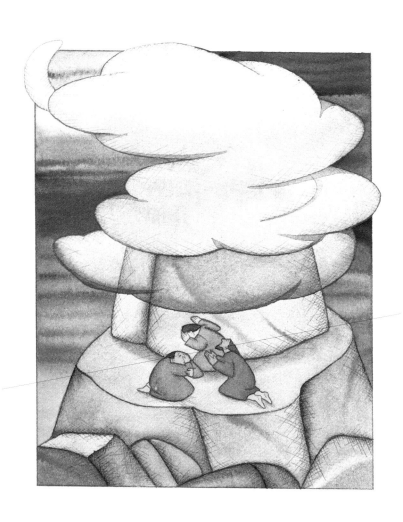

cloud

A **cloud** gathered

and a voice came from out of the cloud,

'This is my beloved son.

Listen to him.'

Mark 9:7

children

People were bringing their **children** to Jesus,

but the disciples hurried them away.

Jesus was angry,

'Let the children come to me,

for the Kingdom of God

belongs to those who are like them.'

Mark 10:13,14

commandments

A man asked Jesus,

'What must I do to have eternal life?'

Jesus said to him,

'You know the **commandments**.

The man replied,

'I have kept them since I was a child.'

Mark 10:17,19,20

treasure in heaven

Then, looking at him hard and long,

Jesus loved him.

He said to him,

'Only one thing is missing.

Go. Sell all you own.

Give the money to the poor and you will have

treasure in heaven.

Then, come and follow me.'

When he heard these words

the man went away sadly,

for he was very rich.

Mark 10:21,22

pray

Jesus said to his disciples,

'When you pray, do not

say the same thing over and over,

because your Father knows what you need.

So **pray** like this,

Our Father in heaven,

Your name is holy.'

Matthew 6:7,8,9

lilies of the field

Jesus also said,

'Why worry about your clothes?

Think about the **lilies of the field**.

They do not work or spin,

but I tell you that Solomon himself

in all his glory was not dressed

as well as one of these.'

Matthew 6:28,29

fruits

'Beware of false prophets.

You will know them by their **fruits**.

A good tree cannot bear evil fruit,

nor can a bad tree bear good fruit.'

Matthew 7:15,16,18

rock

'Everyone who listens

to what I am telling you

and who does as I say

is like a man

who built his house on **rock**.

The rain fell,

the floods came,

the storm raged,

but the house did not fall.'

Matthew 7:24,25

sand

'Everyone who listens to these words
of mine and does not do them is like a man
who built his house on the **sand**.
The rain fell, the floods came,
the storm raged and the house fell down.'

Matthew 7:26,27

lake

Jesus was sitting by the side of the **lake**.

The whole crowd stood on the bank.

He told them many things in parables.

Matthew 13:1,2,3

seed

The Kingdom of Heaven

is like a mustard **seed**

which a man sows in his field.

It is the smallest of all seeds.

Matthew 13:31,32

87

tree

It grows into a **tree**

so big that the birds of the sky

make their nests

in its branches.

Matthew 13:32

treasure

The Kingdom of Heaven is like

treasure hidden in a field.

The man who discovers it

goes and sells everything he has

and goes out and buys that field.

Matthew 13:44

sheep

If a man has a hundred **sheep**

and one of them wanders off,

will he not leave the others to go to search

for the one that is missing?

In the same way, God in heaven does

not want any of his little ones to be lost.

Matthew 18:12,14

well

Jesus arrived in a town in Samaria.

Jacob's **well** was there and, as he was tired,

he sat at the edge of the well.

A woman of Samaria came to draw

some water.

John 4:5,6,7

living water

Jesus said to her,

'Give me something to drink.'

The Samaritan woman said to him,

'Why are you asking me for a drink?'

Jesus replied,

'If you knew who it is who says

to you, "give me something to drink",

then you would have asked him and

he would have given you **living water**.'

John 4:7,9,10

spring of water

Jesus also said,

'Whoever drinks the water which I give

will never be thirsty again.

And the water which I give

will become a **spring of water** welling up

for eternal life.'

John 4:14

the Law

A lawyer asked Jesus,

'What must I do to have eternal life?'

Jesus asked him,

'What is written in **the Law**?'

The man replied,

'You will love the Lord your God

with all your heart, with all your soul,

with all your strength,

and with all your mind,

and your neighbour as yourself.'

Luke 10:25,26,27

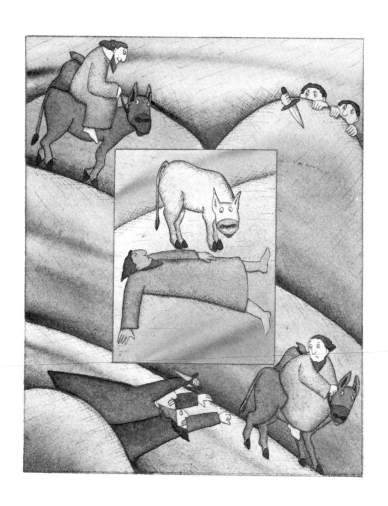

thieves

Jesus said to him,

'You have answered well.

Do this and you will have life.'

But the man said to Jesus,

'But who, then, is my neighbour?'

Jesus continued,

'A man was going down from Jerusalem to Jericho and he fell among **thieves** who left him half dead.'

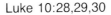

Luke 10:28,29,30

care

'A priest was going down this road.

He saw him and passed by on the other side.

A Samaritan saw him, went up to him,

bound up his wounds and led him to an inn

and took **care** of him.'

Luke 10:31,33,34

neighbour

'Which of these, do you think,

was a **neighbour** to the man

who had fallen into the hands of thieves?'

The lawyer replied,

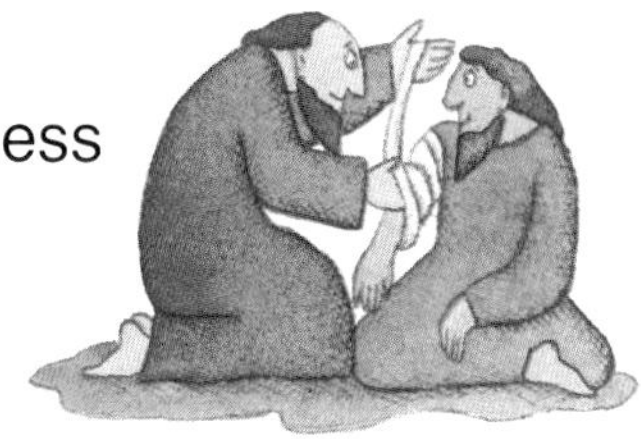

'The one who showed goodness

towards him.'

Jesus said,

'Go, and do the same yourself.'

Luke 10:36,37

preparations

Jesus went into a village.

A woman called Martha welcomed him into

her house.

Her sister, Mary,

sitting at the feet of the Lord,

listened to his words.

Martha was busy with all the **preparations**.

Luke 10:38,39,40

best part

Martha said to Jesus,

'My sister is leaving me to do all the

work alone.

Tell her to help me.'

The Lord replied to her,

'Martha, you are worried about many things.

Only one is necessary.

Mary has chosen the **best part**.'

Luke 10:40,41,42

sycamore

Jesus was passing through the city of Jericho.

Now, Zacchaeus, the chief tax collector,

was there.

He was trying to see who Jesus was.

As he was quite short he climbed into a

sycamore to see him better.

Luke 19:1,2,3,4

house

Jesus looked up,

'Zacchaeus, come down, quickly.

I must come and stay at your house.'

He got down quickly and received

Jesus joyfully.

Jesus said,

'Today salvation has come to this **house**.'

Luke 19:5,6,9

blind

Jesus was leaving Jericho with his disciples.

A **blind** beggar, Bartimaeus, son of Timaeus,

was sitting by the side of the road.

He called out,

'Jesus, son of David. Have mercy on me.'

Mark 10:46,47

way

Jesus stopped and said,

'Call him.'

The blind man leapt

towards Jesus.

Jesus said to him,

'Go, your faith has

saved you.'

Straight away, the man could

see again and he followed

Jesus along the **way**.

Mark 10:49,50,52

donkey

Jesus and his disciples

approached Jerusalem.

Jesus sent off two of his disciples.

'You will find a small **donkey**.

Bring it here.'

They led the little donkey to Jesus.

Mark 11:1,2,7

branches

Jesus sat on the little donkey.

Then many people spread their

cloaks on the road, and others spread

out **branches** cut from the

countryside.

Mark 11:7,8

hosanna

They cried out,

'**Hosanna**!

Blessed be he who comes

in the name of the Lord.

Blessed be the kingdom

which is coming,

the Kingdom of David,

our father.'

Mark 11:9,10

merchants

Jesus went into the Temple

and drove out the **merchants**,

the people who were selling

and those who were buying in the Temple.

After that he said to the people,

'My house will be called the House of Prayer

for all nations.

You have made it

a den of thieves.'

Mark 11:15,17

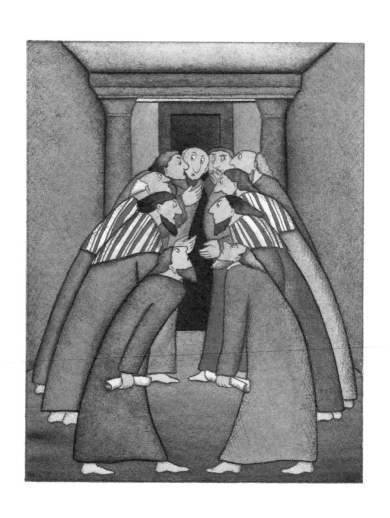

murder

The Chief Priests and the scribes

heard this and they looked for

a way to **murder** him.

Mark 11:18

betray

It was time for the feast of the Passover

to take place.

When evening came,

Jesus arrived with the twelve.

While they were sitting at the table eating,

Jesus said to them,

'One of you is going to **betray** me.'

One after another they asked him sadly,

'Will it be me?'

Mark 14:1,17,18,19

bread

During the meal, Jesus took **bread**,

spoke the blessing,

broke it and gave it to them saying,

'Take, this is my body.'

Mark 14:22

cup

Then, taking the **cup** and giving thanks

he gave it to them and they all drank from it.

He said to them,

'This is my blood.

I tell you,

I will never again drink of the fruit of the vine

until the day when I will drink a new wine

in the Kingdom of God.'

Mark 14:23,24,25

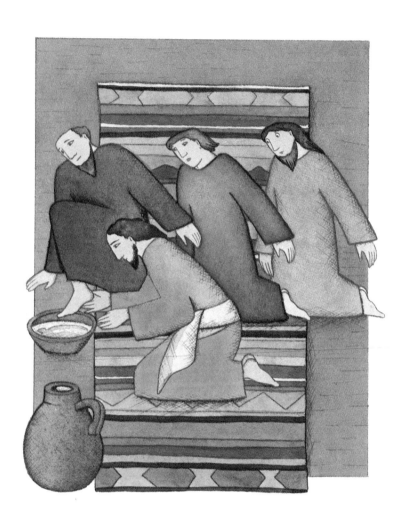

feet

During the meal,

Jesus rose from the table

and took a cloth

which he knotted round his waist.

Then he poured some water into a basin,

started to wash the **feet** of the disciples

and to dry them with the cloth.

He said to them,

'You, also,

should do as I have done for you.'

John 13:2,4,5,12,15

garden

Jesus went out and crossed the Kidron Valley.

There was a **garden** there,

which he went into with his disciples.

John 18:1

soldiers

Judas knew the place.

So he took a band of **soldiers** with him

and some guards

sent by the Chief Priests

and the pharisees.

Then the soldiers seized and bound Jesus.

John 18:2,3,12

high priest

They led him first to the house

of the **High Priest**.

He questioned Jesus.

John 18:13,19

no

As it was cold,

the servants and the guards

had lit a fire to warm themselves.

Peter was with them and was warming himself

as well.

They said to him,

'Are you one of the disciples, too?'

He replied,

'**No**. I am not one of them.'

John 18:18,25

crown of thorns

They led Jesus to the governor, Pilate.

He said to them,

'I do not find any reason to condemn him.

Do you want me to release him?'

They shouted,

'Not him! Barabbas!'

So Pilate ordered that they should

bring Jesus and have him flogged.

The soldiers put a **crown of thorns**

on his head.

John 18:28,38,39,40
John 19:1,2

cross

When they saw him,

the Chief Priests and the guards

started to shout,

'Crucify him. Crucify him.'

Jesus, carrying his **cross** himself,

went out to the place called Golgotha.

There, they crucified him

and two others with him.

After that,

knowing that everything had been done,

Jesus, bowing his head,

gave up his spirit.

John 19:6,17,18,28,30

body

Joseph of Arimathea,

who was a disciple of Jesus,

asked Pilate if he could take away

the **body** of Jesus.

Nicodemus also came with him.

They wrapped him in a shroud.

Near to the place where Jesus had been

crucified there was a new tomb.

They laid Jesus there.

John 19:38,39,40,41,42

morning

On the first day of the week,

Mary Magdalene went to the tomb

very early in the **morning**.

She saw that the stone had been

rolled away from the tomb.

So she ran to find Simon Peter

and the other disciple, the one Jesus loved,

and she said to them,

'They have taken the Lord

from his tomb

and we do not know

where they have laid him.'

John 20:1,2

tomb

So Peter and the other disciple

left to go to the **tomb**.

Peter went into the tomb

and looked at the shroud lying there.

Then the other disciple went in.

He saw and he believed.

Until then the disciples had not understood

that, according to the Scripture,

Jesus had to rise from the dead.

John 20:3,6,8,9

rabboni

Mary Magdalene stayed outside,

crying in front of the tomb.

Jesus was there and she saw him,

but she did not recognise him.

Then Jesus said to her,

'Mary!'

She turned towards him and said,

'**Rabboni!**' which means 'Master'.

Then Mary Magdalene went off to tell the

other disciples,

'I have seen the Lord.'

John 20:11,14,16,18

joy

The eleven disciples and their companions
met together.

Jesus himself stood among them and he
said to them,

'Peace be with you.'

Then he led them out as far as Bethany.

While he was blessing them he left them
and was carried up to heaven.

They fell down and worshipped him,

and then returned to Jerusalem filled

with **joy**.

Luke 24:36,50,51,52

fire

When the Feast of Pentecost
arrived they were all gathered together.
Suddenly, a noise like a violent gust of
wind came from heaven.
They saw something like **fire**.
Then they were all filled with the
Holy Spirit.

Acts 2:1,2,3,4

message

When the people heard the noise,

they gathered together in a crowd.

Peter, standing up with the eleven

other apostles, started to speak.

He said,

'People of Israel.

Listen to this **message**.

It is about Jesus of Nazareth.

God has raised him up and made him

the Lord, the Christ.'

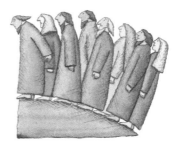

Acts 2:6,14,22,32,36

promise

Those that heard him said to Peter
and the other apostles,
'Brothers, what must we do?'
Peter replied,
'Let everyone be baptized in the name of
Jesus Christ. Then you will
receive the gift of the Holy Spirit.
It is for you that God has made this
promise, and for all those whom the Lord
our God will call.'

Acts 2:37,38,39

Stories from the New Testament

The Birth of Jesus

Mary was only a young girl. One day, a stranger appeared in front of her. 'Who are you?' she asked.

'Don't worry,' he said. 'It's all right.'

'Oh?'

'Yes.'

He was beautiful. The loveliest thing she had ever seen, so she trusted him.

'You're going to have a baby,' he told her.

Mary wasn't so sure about this. 'Why?'

'God wants you to. But only if you want.'

'Well, if God wants me to,' she said, 'It's all right with me.'

'That's good,' said the angel. 'I'll be off then.'

'Oh, dear,' said Mary. She really liked the angel and was sad he was going. 'Is that all?'

'More or less,' he said. 'Call the baby Jesus.'

In the end it wasn't at all how Mary thought it would be. They had to go a long way away, right down to the South to Bethlehem, where Joseph came from.

'Are you all right?' Joseph asked her about a hundred times a day while they were travelling. She always smiled when he asked her. 'All right,' she said. But it was hard going.

And then, when they got to Bethlehem, there wasn't anywhere at all to sleep, so they had to make beds in a stable, with all the animals, in there.

'Still,' said Joseph. 'It's cosy.' And it was.

When the baby was born that night, in the stable, Mary made him a special little bed in the manger. She thought the lovely angel had forgotten all about her. But, that night, he woke up some shepherds who were in the fields just near by.

'Come on,' he said.

'That's an angel,' said one of the shepherds.

'No,' said another.

'Must be,' said a third.

The angel hurried them up. 'There isn't time to stand around arguing,' he said. 'I've got the best news you'll ever hear. Go to Bethlehem. Look for the baby in the manger.'

'Why?'

'Because,' the angel explained, 'he is the Saviour, the Messiah.'

So, off they went, and Mary was very glad to see them and know that the angel was still thinking about her.

The Wise Men

Some very wise men saw a special star in the sky.

'Let's follow it,' said one.

'See where it leads,' said another.

So off they went. They travelled miles and miles from the east until they arrived at Jerusalem.

'Better go to ask the King,' said the first one. So they went to King Herod. They told him a new king had been born.

King Herod pretended to be glad to see them. 'A new king?' he asked.

'That's what the star means,' explained the wise men.

'Oh, good,' he said, but he was lying. He liked being king and didn't want a new one coming along. 'Have a look in Bethlehem,' he said. 'Tell me if you find him.'

'Of course. Thank you,' they said.

They found Jesus and gave him presents: gold and lovely incense and myrrh.

'Thank you,' said Mary.

The angel hadn't forgotten the new baby. He told the wise men in a dream that they had better not tell Herod after all. 'You never know,' he said. So they didn't.

Simeon

Mary and Joseph took the baby Jesus to the Temple in Jerusalem to show him to God and to say thank you for him. There was an old man there called Simeon. He held the baby. 'This is a very special baby,' he told Mary. Mary was very pleased at this. 'He will show many wonderful things.' Mary smiled. 'But,' the man went on, 'he will also destroy many things.'

'Oh dear,' said Mary.

'Don't worry though,' said Simeon. 'They will only be things that need to be destroyed.'

'Good,' said Mary.

'But he will make you suffer as though a sword were pushed into your heart.'

'Yes,' said Mary. 'That's babies all right.' And they took Jesus home and he grew up to be a fine boy.

Jesus in the Temple

When Jesus was twelve Mary and Joseph took him to Jerusalem for the pilgrimage. It was a wonderful time, with all their family and friends from Nazareth. They all travelled there together and then back again. It wasn't until they were quite a long way back towards home that Mary noticed that Jesus wasn't anywhere around.

'No,' said everyone. 'We thought he was with you.'

'And I thought he was with you,' she said.

'Come on,' said Joseph. 'We'll go back and look for him.' They stayed calm, but they were both very worried. They looked for ages. In the end they found him in the Temple, talking to all the clever lawyers and teachers.

'There you are,' said Mary.

'Of course,' said Jesus. 'I'm in my Father's house.'

Mary was too relieved to be angry, and she was surprised to see how the clever men were listening to her small boy.

John the Baptist

The years passed. Jesus grew up to be a man and he worked at Joseph's business as a carpenter.

Out in the desert people went in great crowds to see a strange man who was teaching new things. He was called John and was Jesus' cousin. People called him the Baptist because he took them into the river Jordan and plunged them into the water to wash away their sins. He wore rough clothes, ate whatever he could find in the desert and he had never shaved or had his hair cut. He looked very wild and fierce. People thought he was a great man.

'Don't you believe it,' John said to them. 'There's someone coming who is much greater than I am.' This made the people more excited than ever. Jesus went to see John in the desert.

'That's the one,' said John, pointing at Jesus. 'I told you he would come.'

'Baptize me,' Jesus said to him.

John didn't want to. 'You baptize me,' he said to Jesus.

'Come on,' Jesus insisted. 'Let's get on with it.' So John baptized him and when Jesus came up out of the water they all felt a wonderful, light, fluttering feeling, like a dove in flight. It was the Holy Spirit blessing Jesus. And there was a voice which said, 'This is my son, my beloved.'

The Twelve Disciples

Jesus started to gather some friends who could help him. He met two men fishing on the Sea of Galilee. 'Wouldn't you rather catch men for God?' he asked them. Jesus liked a joke and they laughed too. 'All right,' they said. And they left their nets and went with him. Jesus chose some more people until there were twelve altogether. 'That'll do,' said Jesus. 'Let's get to work.'

The Marriage at Cana

Jesus was at a wedding at Cana-in-Galilee with his mother. Mary was still very proud of him and she never forgot the angel. During the meal the wine ran out.

'Do what he tells you,' Mary told the servants, pointing at Jesus.

Jesus told the servants to fill up some big stone jars with water. They were special jars, used by the Jews to wash themselves clean from sins.

'Take some water out of the jars now and give it to the man in charge,' he said. The servants shrugged their shoulders and thought Jesus was a bit strange, but they didn't like to argue.

The man in charge tasted it and said, 'This is the best wine I've ever had.' All the jars were full of it.

Mary remembered that Simeon had said Jesus was going to change lots of things.

'Well,' she thought. 'It's started.'

The Paralytic

After this Jesus became quite famous. Sometimes people couldn't get near enough to him because of the crowds. One day, Jesus was in a house and four men carried a paralysed friend to see him, but they could not get near at all. So they climbed up the side of the house and took the roof off and lowered their friend down, right in front of Jesus.

'Get up,' said Jesus. 'Then you can carry your stretcher out the proper way.' They were all astonished when the man got up and could walk.

The Family of Jesus

One day when Jesus was busy his mother and his brothers arrived. The disciples called over to Jesus to let him know.

'Who's here?' asked Jesus.

'Your mother and your brothers,' they said.

'Anyone who does what God wants is my mother and my brother and my sister,' said Jesus.

Mary felt a small stab at her heart when she heard this.

The Storm

One evening the disciples were out in their boat when they saw Jesus by the shore. He joined them in the boat and fell asleep on a cushion in the stern. A sudden storm started and the boat rocked violently, and water came in over the side. The disciples were frightened and woke Jesus up. He stood up, turned his face into the wind and shouted at it.

'That's enough,' he yelled. 'Stop it.'

The storm stopped suddenly and everything was calm. The disciples looked at each other. 'How can he do that?' they wondered. 'Who is he?'

The Feeding of the Five Thousand

There always seemed to be crowds wanting to see Jesus and to hear him. One day the disciples said, 'Look, everyone's hungry. Send them off to get something to eat.' There were thousands of people. 'Where?' said Jesus. 'They'll never find anything. What have we got?' The disciples found five little loaves and two fishes. 'That's all,' they said. 'What good is that for such a lot of people?'

'Let's see,' said Jesus. He took the bread, lifted up his eyes, thanked God for the food, broke the bread and passed it around. There was enough food for everyone, and when they had all had enough to eat the disciples picked up the scraps that were left and they filled twelve big baskets.

The Transfiguration

Jesus took Peter and James and John and they climbed a mountain together. Jesus went ahead of them right to the top.

'Look,' said Peter. As they looked at Jesus

he seemed quite different and very special. His clothes shone with a bright light. Then a cloud came down and covered everything and a voice came out of the cloud, 'This is my son, my beloved. Listen to him.'

The Kingdom of Heaven

People wanted their children to see Jesus. There were hordes of them running around, squealing and singing. This annoyed the disciples.

'Get them away,' they said. 'Jesus is a very important person.'

'Oh,' said Jesus. 'Don't do that. Everyone has to be like a little child. It's the only way to get into the Kingdom of Heaven.'

More and more people came to ask Jesus things. Once, a very rich man asked him, 'How can I have eternal life?'

'Well,' said Jesus. 'Do you know the commandments?'

The man was a bit cross. He wanted something new and special from Jesus.

'Of course I do,' he said. 'And I have kept them since I was a little child.'

Even when people were touchy with Jesus he still loved them and now he looked at this man and loved him, so he told him something very special.

'All right, then. Sell everything you own. Give the money to the poor, then come and follow me. You don't need all those things. You can have treasure in Heaven.'

But the man grew very sad and went away from Jesus because he was very rich and he didn't want to give his things away.

'Always talk to God,' Jesus told his disciples. 'And don't be afraid of him. Tell him everything because he loves you. Think of how a good father looks after his little children. Say to God – Our Father in Heaven, even your name is holy.'

Parables

Jesus still liked jokes. It was hard work on the road, teaching people and healing them. They got messy and ragged. 'Don't worry,' laughed Jesus. He showed them the poppies in the fields and the flowers growing by the side of the road. 'Look at these beautiful flowers,' he said. 'They don't do anything to make their clothes, but even King Solomon was never dressed as well as them.'

There were lots of other people like Jesus, talking about God and telling people what God was like and what God wanted them to do. 'Better be careful,' Jesus warned people. 'You never know. The best way to see whether someone is teaching you the right thing is to see whether what they do is good or bad. It's like a tree, isn't it? You don't get good fruit from a bad tree.'

Jesus was always telling little stories like that. People loved to hear them, and then they thought about what the story meant.

'If a man builds a house on sand,' he said, 'and the wind blows and the rain falls, it will all be washed away. Listen to my words and do them. Then you will be like a man who builds his house on a rock. When the wind blows and the rain beats down you will be safe inside.'

Everyone laughed when they thought of the house on the sand, but they remembered what he said about his words and how they should do them.

Jesus told lots of these stories.

'What's the Kingdom of Heaven like?' they asked.

'Like a mustard seed. It's so tiny when you first see it that you can hardly believe it could be worth anything. But when you plant it it grows into a tree big enough for the birds to build their nests in.'

'It's like a treasure chest hidden in a field. When you see how valuable it is you sell everything to buy the field and own the treasure.'

'Do you know how much God loves you?'

he asked. 'Suppose a man had one hundred sheep and he lost one and went off to look for it to bring it back to the rest. That's how much God loves you.'

Jesus went to a town in Samaria and sat next to the Well of Jacob. When a woman came to get some water he asked her for a drink. Jews and Samaritans don't get on together and they don't share the same cups or plates so she was very surprised. She asked Jesus what he meant. Jesus said, 'If you knew who I am you would ask me and I would give water for everlasting life.'

The Good Samaritan

Some people didn't like Jesus at all. They were frightened of him and they tried to trap him. One man, a lawyer, asked Jesus, 'What do I have to do to have eternal life?'

Jesus always liked a joke so he teased the man. 'You're the lawyer,' he said. 'What does the law say?'

The man said, 'Love God with all your heart and with all your soul and with all your strength and with all your mind, and love your neighbour as yourself.'

'Good,' said Jesus. 'Just do that, then.'

But the man still wanted to trap him, so he asked him, 'But who is my neighbour?'

Jesus thought it was time for another story. 'A man went from Jerusalem to Jericho. He was attacked by thieves on the way and beaten up, robbed and left for dead. A priest came along and saw the man but he ignored him and went past. Then a Samaritan came along.' Jesus smiled when he said this because the lawyer hated the Samaritans. 'The Samaritan stopped, even though the robbers might still be around. He bound up the man's wounds, gave him a drink, put him on his own donkey and took him to an inn. He paid all the bills himself. Which of these people do you think was the neighbour to the man who was attacked?'

The lawyer was annoyed because he had fallen into his own trap. 'The Samaritan,' he said.

'Go away and be like a Samaritan, then,' said Jesus. Everyone laughed, except the lawyer.

Mary and Martha

Jesus went to stay with his friends Mary and Martha. Martha fussed around getting food ready and tidying up. She was very busy. Mary sat with Jesus, listening to him and enjoying being with him. At last Martha exploded.

'Tell Mary to come and help me,' she said, 'I'm doing everything.'

'Come on, Martha,' said Jesus gently. 'You don't need to be so busy. Sit and be still with me like Mary. She's made a better choice.'

Zacchaeus

When Jesus was going through Jericho there was a man called Zacchaeus who wanted to see him. Everyone hated Zacchaeus because he was a tax collector and he cheated people out of their money. They wouldn't let him get to the front of the crowd to see Jesus and he was so short that he couldn't see over their heads. So he climbed up into a sycamore tree to get a better view. Jesus saw him there and he looked so funny that Jesus laughed and shouted out to him, 'Come on, Zacchaeus. Get down. I'm coming to eat at your house today.'

So Zacchaeus scrambled down and ran off to get things ready. When Jesus got there Zacchaeus said, 'I'm going to pay back all the people I've cheated and I'm not going to cheat any more.'

'Good,' said Jesus. 'Today salvation has come to your house.'

Blind Bartimaeus

Jesus left Jericho and a blind beggar called

Bartimaeus shouted out to him from the roadside, 'Jesus, son of David. Have mercy on me.'

Jesus did not smile at all. Sometimes things were very serious and now they seemed to get more serious all the time. 'Bring him here,' he said to his disciples.

'Your faith has saved you,' he said to Bartimaeus and Bartimaeus could see again. He followed Jesus along the way.

The Triumphal Entry into Jerusalem

As they drew near to Jerusalem Jesus said to his disciples, 'You will find a little donkey. Bring him to me.'

So they brought the donkey to Jesus and he rode him into the city. People spread out their cloaks for Jesus to ride on, and they cut palm branches and spread them out as well, and they sang a psalm about the king coming into his city and they all sang 'Hosannah'.

Jesus went straight to the Temple and he took the tables that the money changers used and he threw them about. Then he made a whip and beat the money changers with it and drove them out.

'You're all cheats,' he shouted. 'And swindlers. And this Temple is to be a place of prayer.' The Chief Priests were furious and they got together to work out a way to murder him.

The Last Supper

When the Feast of the Passover arrived Jesus met with his twelve disciples.

'One of you is going to betray me,' he said. Jesus was very serious.

The disciples all asked, 'Will it be me?'

During the meal Jesus took some bread. He raised his eyes to heaven, gave thanks to God for the food, broke the bread and passed it to his disciples.

'This is my body,' he said.

Then he took the cup and gave thanks. He gave it to them and said, 'This is my blood. I give you this so that your sins may be forgiven.'

He left the table, took a cloth and knotted it around his waist and started to wash the feet of the disciples.

'Not me,' said Peter. 'You can't wash my feet.' He thought Jesus was too great a man to wash feet.

'All right, then,' said Jesus. 'But you're nothing to do with me if I don't.'

So Peter knew he had done something stupid and said, 'Wash my feet, my head, hands, everything.'

Jesus said to all of them, 'You must be servants like this.'

The Garden of Gethsemane

Then they all left the house and went with Jesus to a garden. Judas brought some soldiers with him, showed them who Jesus was by kissing him and the soldiers arrested Jesus. They took him to the High Priest who was to ask Jesus questions to prove that he should die.

The disciples ran away afraid. Peter hid in a courtyard and warmed himself by a fire. But a servant girl said, 'You were with Jesus, weren't you?'

'No,' said Peter.

'Yes you were.'

Peter denied it again.

The Chief Priests took Jesus to Pontius Pilate the Roman Governor. He tried to let Jesus go but they stopped him. So Pilate let them take Jesus away and torture him. They put a crown of thorns on his head.

The Crucifiction

When the Chief Priests took him out, all the people shouted out, 'Crucify him. Crucify him.'

They made Jesus carry a heavy cross out of the city to a place called Golgotha. There they nailed him to the cross and crucified him with two other men on their crosses. At last Jesus called out that he had done the work he had come to do and that he was ready to go back to God, and he died.

Mary was there, at the foot of the cross. She looked at Jesus suffering and it was as though a sword went through her heart.

The Resurrection

There was a follower of Jesus called Joseph of Arimathea who went to Pilate and asked if he could take the body of Jesus to bury it. Pilate gave him permission. Near to where he had been crucified there was a garden, with a new tomb that had never been used before. They took the body of Jesus there and wrapped it in spices and in a shroud and laid it there. A huge stone was placed over the entrance to the tomb.

On the first day of the week Mary Magdalene went to the garden where the tomb was. She saw that the stone had been rolled away. She ran off to find Peter and John.

'They've taken him away,' she said. 'He's gone.'

They all ran together to see what had happened. Peter got there first and went into the tomb. Then John went in. They saw that it was empty and they understood that the body of Jesus had not been stolen away but that he had risen from the dead.

Mary Magdalene was standing in the garden, outside the tomb. She was crying. A man was there and he said to her, 'Mary.' Mary said, 'Oh, master,' when she saw that it was Jesus. She rushed off to tell the other disciples what had happened.

The Ascension

They all met together and Jesus appeared in front of them and said, 'Peace be with you.'

They thought that Jesus would stay with them always now, but he took the disciples to Bethany. He blessed them, and then he was taken away from them to Heaven. They knelt down and they lay on the ground and worshipped him. Then they went back to Jerusalem and were not sad any more but were full of joy.

The Good News

Not long afterwards, on the Feast of Pentecost, the disciples were alone together. They were frightened that they might be put to death like Jesus had been so they had locked the doors. Suddenly, there was an enormous blast of wind. Then, they saw tongues of fire licking round. Even so, all their fear left them.

'Out!' shouted Peter. 'Outside.'

They all ran out and started to tell people about how Jesus had risen from the dead. Everyone was really excited.

'Look,' someone said. 'They're drunk.'

The disciples laughed and laughed. It was just like one of the jokes that Jesus told.

'We're not drunk,' said Peter. 'We're filled with the Holy Spirit.'

'What do we have to do to be so happy, and to have eternal life?' people asked them.

'Be baptized,' said Peter. 'Receive the Holy Spirit. Believe in Jesus.'

Index of Biblical References

Index

The figures refer to words in the illustrated section of the book (pp. 6 to 167).

How to Use This Book with Children

This book is a book of images of the Bible that you can read with children and discuss each word, each picture and each extract. The illustrations will inspire you to tell the stories about Jesus and his life, following the Gospels of the New Testament – the feeding of the five thousand and the Last Supper or the healing of the blind man, the Transfiguration and the Resurrection. You could also take certain words and pictures and use them as a special text or prayer for a child.

Let your children open the book themselves and choose the words and pictures they like. They can then retell the stories to you in their own words. You can also refer to the back of the book where the best known stories from the Gospels are retold for children and read them aloud together.

As you use this book you will discover thousands of different ways to read this first Bible and make it a very special introduction to the Scriptures for your children.

Imprimé en France par Aubin Imprimeur, Ligugé, Poitiers